For Nora—J.K.

For My Mother—S.G.

Copyright © 1994 by Jill Kearney
Illustrations Copyright © 1994 by Simon Galkin

Published by Longmeadow Press, 201 High Ridge Road, Stamford, CT 06904. All rights reserved. No part of this book may be reproduced or utilized in any form or by any means, electronic or mechanical, including photocopying, recording or by any information storage and retrieval system, without permission in writing from the Publisher.
Longmeadow Press and the colophon are registered trademarks.

Book design by Allison G. Russo

Printed in Singapore
First Longmeadow Press Edition
0 9 8 7 6 5 4 3 2 1

Library of Congress Cataloging-in-Publication Data

Kearney, Jill.
A Fishmas carol / by Jill Kearney. — 1st ed.
p.   cm.
ISBN 0-681-00582-3
1. Marine fauna—Juvenile poetry. 2. Santa Claus—Juvenile
poetry. 3. Christmas—Juvenile poetry. 4. Children's poetry,
American.   I. Title.
PS3561.E2438F57   1994
811'.54—dc20   94-6198
                                 CIP
                                 AC

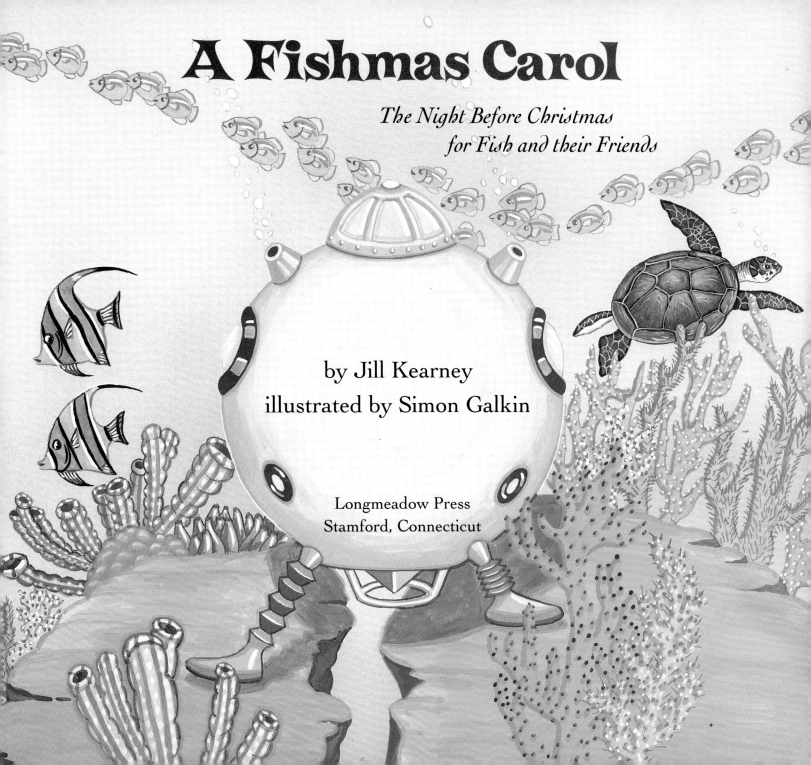

A Fishmas Carol

The Night Before Christmas
for Fish and their Friends

by Jill Kearney

illustrated by Simon Galkin

Longmeadow Press
Stamford, Connecticut

'Twas the night before Christmas and all through the ocean
Not a creature was making the slightest commotion.

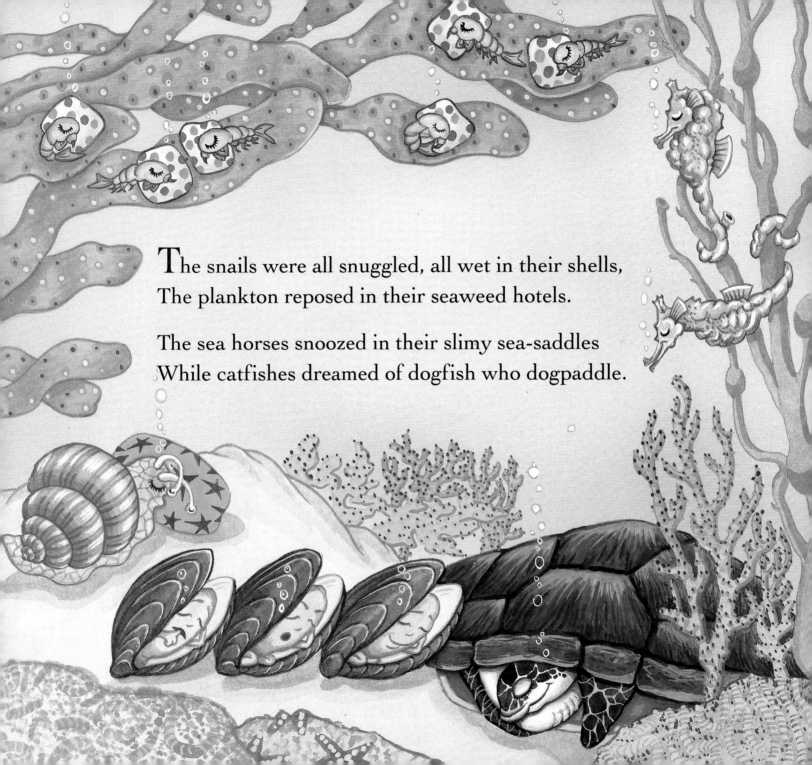

The snails were all snuggled, all wet in their shells,
The plankton reposed in their seaweed hotels.

The sea horses snoozed in their slimy sea-saddles
While catfishes dreamed of dogfish who dogpaddle.

Mama in her scuba, and I, in my sub
Had just settled in for some fine deep-sea grub,

When all of a sudden from out of the kelp
Came twelve sinking reindeer
and a man screaming "Help!"

"Merry Christmas to all!" he said with a grin,
"Merry Christmas to all!" and then, "Help! I can't swim!"

His jovial face was as pink as a rose.
As he struggled for breath three fish swam up his nose.

His suit was all soaked from his stem to his stern,
And I knew in a flash there was much I could learn.

For despite his misfortune he seemed in good mood
As he gave out gift baskets of gourmet fish food.

There were minnows and sand crabs wrapped up in his beard
And exactly the kind of moray eel I feared!

But instead of recoiling from said scary eel—
He presented the fish with a new rod and reel!

He spoke not a word, but went straight to his mission,
And gave the glowworms books on nuclear fission.

He gave all the bluefish an autographed book
And he gave alligators the bio on Hook.

The seahorses walked off with shiny new spurs.
He gave the clams monogrammed towels, his and hers.

By now he was turning a pale shade of blue,
And the thought dawned on me there was much I could do.

I tethered the fat man up tight to my craft,
And the twelve sinking reindeer, and surfaced them aft.

Then I asked the fat man– "Are you someone I know?
You look so familiar– Are you Jacques Cousteau?"

To which the fat man replied, "HO HO HO!"

And I heard him exclaim as he hoisted his sails,

"Merry Christmas to all, and please save the whales!"